ORMSKIRK
THROUGH TIME
Mona Duggan

AMBERLEY PUBLISHING

Ormskirk Market in the early twentieth century.

First published 2009

Amberley Publishing Plc
Cirencester Road, Chalford,
Stroud, Gloucestershire, GL6 8PE

www.amberley-books.com

Copyright © Mona Duggan, 2009

The right of Mona Duggan to be identified as the
Author of this work has been asserted in accordance
with the Copyrights, Designs and Patents Act 1988.

ISBN 978 1 84868 674 8

British Library Cataloguing in Publication Data.
A catalogue record for this book is available from
the British Library.

Typeset in 9.5pt on 12pt Celeste.
Typesetting by Amberley Publishing.
Printed in the UK.

Introduction

Sometimes when I look at an old building, I wish the walls could speak and tell me what has happened to the building in the past. I wonder why it was built in that place, what sort of people lived and worked there and what their hopes and dreams were. Of course, buildings cannot be given a voice, but I hope that by looking closely at those featured in this book, their details may reveal how the lifestyle and aspirations of the people of Ormskirk have changed during the last 150 years.

The old photographs in this book date from the nineteenth century when gas lights lit the town and the streets were cobbled to prevent the horses' feet slipping as they pulled their heavy loads through the narrow streets. Pedestrianisation was a thing of the future and its introduction has made such a difference to the town. Health and safety were not on the agenda at that time, and as we look at the views of Burscough Street with heavy lorries wending their way among the crowds, we cannot help cringing in fear of an accident waiting to happen. The living conditions portrayed in some of the photographs also fill us with horror. How could those little children live in such cramped courtyards with primitive sanitary arrangements?

The coloured photographs emphasise the changes; in some cases they chart the actual building operations as the old Ormskirk was transformed into the town we know today. The photos reveal which changes the townsfolk regarded as important and which conditions they accepted without question. A closer look at the buildings shows that many of the alterations were only superficial and much of the old town remains concealed under a thin veil of 'improvements'.

Edge Hill University.

Nevertheless large areas have been cleared and new buildings erected. The town can be proud of many of these and can celebrate the transformation that has taken place. However, there are changes that many regret, such as the demolition of the Kings Arms and its substitution with the Boots building. Yet a glimpse of the old cottages in Green Lane and the courts behind Church Street and Aughton Street show how much the town has changed for the better. The disappearance of the small shops is compensated for by the arrival of the large supermarkets, where all the shopping can be done at once without the hassle and weariness of trekking from one shop to another carrying an ever-increasing load.

Behind the façades of the buildings are the people of Ormskirk. Sometimes they emerge in their fine hats and long gowns and sometimes we are left to imagine what kind of people they must have been. Many of those who read this book will have known them and the book will thus rekindle memories of happy times in the past. That is my hope as I take you through Ormskirk, starting from the clock tower in the centre of the town.

Mona Duggan, 2009

Moor Street

A Busy Market Place

The Kings Arms dominated the centre of Ormskirk during the early twentieth century. Election results were declared from its balcony, and several famous people appeared there to wave to the crowds. Traditionally the annual fair took place in front of the hotel, but the cattle market had to be moved to the eastern end of Moor Street because of the disruption it caused. The hotel was demolished in the 1950s and replaced by these shops.

Alongside the Kings Arms

The building alongside the Kings
Arms was Wainwright's ironmongers
shop before it was converted into the
canopied corn exchange. Between
that building and Swift's café was
Market Row. When the Midland
Bank was built, Market Row became
a small footpath, which was closed
when the Wheatsheaf car park was
developed. The Midland Bank became
the HSBC Bank and Currys now
stands at the corner of the old street.

Celebrations in Town

Most of the festivities that took place in Ormskirk used to be held near the Kings Arms. Here a procession commemorating some national event is seen passing the hotel and the corn exchange. The flags and the style of dress suggest that it was organised to celebrate the coronation of George V. Nowadays the site is still the centre for various displays, such as those given by the local morris dancers.

Tearooms and Cafés

The townsfolk have always enjoyed meeting in a tearoom for a chat and something to eat or drink. In the past a favourite rendezvous was Swift's café, where a 'tea and smoke room' was advertised on the blind above the window. Certainly the smoke room would not be allowed today. Now that more people travel to the continent, fashion has dictated that a pavement café is an attractive alternative — and global warming makes it possible.

Change Taking Place

The adjoining property was demolished and it seemed that Swift's building would remain intact. That was not to be. However, the developer who rebuilt that store retained the stone plaque from over the upper windows and made a feature both of it and the tall gable-end frontage in the new building. The shop to the right with the two bay windows in the upper floor survived and remains today.

The Growth of Taylor's

Barbara Bampton and Dorothy Seddon stand proudly before the doorway of Pooles, the long-established printers, where they also sold leather goods and presents. When that shop closed, Taylor's expanded to sell fancy goods, creating the large store that we have today. Later Taylor's incorporated a café that now is appreciated by those who visit the market.

The Seventeenth-Century Properties

The map of Ormskirk 1609 shows several properties built with the gable end to the road and it is possible that the present shops date from that time. Although the interiors and frontages have been modernised, the basis of the property may have remained the same.

A Parade in Old Moor Street

In this wonderful view we can identify many of the shops and offices of the early twentieth century. To the left is the River Plate Fresh Meat Company's shop with gas lamps outside the window to facilitate late-night shopping. Then comes Stretch the auctioneers, Gilbey's wine store and Poole's the printers, with a bay window in the upper storey. Next to the gable-ended buildings comes Nunnerley's, the drapers. The owner, Sergeant Major Nunnerly, survived the infamous Charge of the Light Brigade in the Crimean War. Finally, in the extreme right is the Golden Lion, one of Ormskirk's oldest inns. It was mentioned by Nicholas Blundell, who wrote in his diary in 1715, 'I went to Ormskirk Fair and swaped my Mair Cherry with Robert Bradshaw for his Hors Dick. I drank at the Golden Lyon with Mr Taylor, the watchmaker, Dr Lancaster etc.'

The Institute

Disraeli's statue stood in the centre of the road near the Working Men's Institute and Cocoa Rooms. The institute was built in the nineteenth century to cater for the self-help movement and to give men an alternative meeting place to the public house. Many productions by the Ormskirk Operatic Company were staged in the large hall, and other organisations used the hall for their money-raising efforts. Today the bus station and car park occupy the site.

A Farmhouse in the Town Centre

On the side of the old farmhouse that stood next to the institute was a sign pointing the way to St Helens. In the modern photograph a bus going to St Helens is passing the site of the farmhouse. Originally this part of the town was known as Moor Street End.

Inset: the front of the farmhouse.

The Bus Station Moved Over

When the farmhouse and institute were demolished, the site was used temporarily as a car lot watched over by Disraeli. By this time respect for the politician had faded and the statue's plinth was covered in graffiti. Then the bus station moved from the end of Knowsley Road onto the site, and Ormskirk's information bureau was built nearby.

A View of Disraeli and St Helens Road Taken from the Institute

The grand house on the left was built for the master of the workhouse and later became the surgery of Dr Lax. In the early twentieth century Dr Lax's surgery was converted into two shops, which changed owners several times through the years. They included a fabric and clothes shop, Mahoods and Hesketh and Walkers. Further down the road can be seen the mansion house that may have been the town house of the earls of Derby during the eighteenth century. In the nineteenth century it became the Mansion House Academy where Thomas Harper taught about eighteen boys. The cottage between the two grand houses was converted into Webster's furniture store — now gone — and the Mansion House was split up into a dentist's surgery and private flats.

Looking Towards the Clock Tower

In the upper photo the market is in progress and boys are trying to sell their wares from their baskets or are running errands for the traders. The old Ship Inn was then Ablett's shoe shop, and the property next door had not been altered. Below we can see how the frontages were changed and the nearest shop now has the Ship on its façade despite the fact that the Ship was actually next door.

A Bicycle and Pram Shop

Tony Ireland and his wife Agnes sold prams, nursery equipment and bicycles in their shop between Clucas's and the Golden Lion in the 1950s. That shop has disappeared and in its place is the entrance to the B&M store.

Ormskirk Cyclists in the 1920s

This group had enjoyed a day out on their bicycles and posed for a photo. Whether the girls had been cycling in those enormous hats or whether they had met the boys later for a picnic is not clear, but it was probably the latter. In those days cycling was predominantly a sport for the male sex, and making the picnic was a task for the females; according to the lower photo the same applies today.

Private Houses into Shops

As so often happened, rooms in these two properties that were originally private residences were converted into shop premises. The old sweet and tobacco shop changed owners and was enlarged to become the present cycle shop, while the taxi firm and Bargain Booze moved into the house next door.

The Market Outside Stoker's

In one of the shops in the upper photo was the old-established firm of Stokers that opened their first shop in Burscough Street to sell fabrics and millinery. They moved into the Moor Street shop to expand into selling carpets and floor coverings, and in 1952 they bought the old school in Derby Street, where they now have a large furniture store. This building was then taken by Ladbrokes, the bookmakers.

A 'Red' Takeover

This shop on the corner of Moor Street and Moorgate was Bottomleys for many years and became Evans when it was inherited by the owner's stepson, Mr Evans. The red façade of the modern Home Bargains certainly brightens up a rainy day.

A Sword and an Anvil and Birds of Prey

Before we leave Moor Street, one more glance back to the time when the sword and the anvil were added to the street furniture. However, it was not long before it was decided to move them to the grounds of St. Bede's School. Nowadays the platform serves as a resting place for tired shoppers or as an unusual place for displaying birds of prey, while Disraeli dominates the eastern end of the street.

PAVILION

ORMSKIRK. Tel. 2269 Resident Manager: Arnold Fielding

Week Commencing Monday, NOV. 8th, 1954

MONDAY, TUESDAY & WEDNESDAY

DEAN MARTIN : JERRY LEWIS
JANET LEIGH

IN   Cert. U

LIVING IT UP

IN TECHNICOLOR

THURSDAY, FRIDAY & SATURDAY

ANNE BAXTER : STEVE COCHRAN
LYLE BETTGER

IN   Cert. A

CARNIVAL STORY

IN TECHNICOLOR

MONDAY TO FRIDAY CONTINUOUS from 5.45 p.m.
MATINEES - MONDAY, THURSDAY & SATURDAY at 2.15 SATURDAY at 2.15, 5.45 and 8.0

RICHARD WHEWELL (BOLTON) LTD

Living it up

A title that describes the feelings of those who went to the Pavilion cinema in Moorgate in the old days, and also of those who go to the night club today. The cinema was never luxurious: the double seats were not exactly comfortable — despite their advantages — and the noise of passing trains drowned the soundtrack. Nevertheless the building has always been the venue for an enjoyable night out.

Gone but not Forgotten

The closure of the food market off Moorgate spelt disaster for this green-grocery stallholder. Car parking has taken over where his stand used to be, and a different stallholder now sells fruit and vegetables from a stall in Moor Street.

Church Street

Boots in Church Street
The shop with the door across the corner was originally Wood's, the chemist's. When customers entered that shop a bell that hung above the door rang to alert the shopkeeper. Eventually Boots took over the shop as in this photo. In the later developments the building line remained the same, but the shop doorway was lost.

Development in Progress

It was decided to demolish a section of the lower part of Church Street and replace it with modern shops. The mock-Tudor premises of the *Ormskirk Advertiser* had provided an interesting focus in the old Church Street, but unfortunately workplaces do need modernising.

Sets in Church Street

The prominence of a saddler's shop next to the White Lion is a reminder that the upper photo was taken before the coming of motor vehicles. Saddlers were in great demand when everyone relied on horses for transport. Here the roadway is paved in sets to prevent the horses from slipping on a smooth surface. Recently the sets have been restored to give character to the street. Interestingly, Scott's butchers previously belonged to Hulme, another butcher.

A Shop That Has Become a Legend

Local young boys thought that Mansergh's hardware shop was an Aladdin's cave, for it was where Miss Mansergh — in her brown overall — could find whatever was wanted from the depths of her shop. Next to the butcher's shop was an alleyway that led to the yard where animals were slaughtered and prepared for sale.

John Ball's Iron Foundry

Many railings and manhole covers that are still in use in the district were made at this foundry. There was a great fire here in the 1930s and several scholars at a local school were punished for spending their dinner hour watching the flames. I suppose the truth was that they stayed there too long and were late for lessons. *Inset:* a piece of iron that has recently been found by archaeologists who were excavating at the rear of the site prior to its redevelopment.

The Old Town Hall

This building was erected in 1779 to replace an earlier hall that stood on the same site. The ground floor provided space for two shops and a covered market for the sale of various cereals, while above was the room where the quarter sessions were held. There was also an assembly room on the upper floor. The town hall included the two shops on either side that are now in separate ownership.

Another Favourite Shop

People in Ormskirk still remember Daish's the grocers where bacon was cut exactly as required and every effort was made to satisfy even the most demanding customer. Now the shop caters for very different needs.

The White Lion

Next door to this public house was the sweet shop kept by Miss Mary Ormesher — known as Auntie Polly by the local children. This elderly lady and her sister were murdered in their home in Asmall Lane. It was thought that the only motive could have been robbery, and by the descriptions of the murder scene, it would seem that the two sisters fought grimly to keep their hard-earned cash. No one has been charged with the crime.

An Old Courtyard Development
It is hard to decide exactly where these cottages were, but the roof of the Snigs Foot brewery can be seen over their roofs, so it would seem that it was the site adjoining the Stiles car park, that is now undeveloped and neglected.

The Civic Dignitaries on Parade

Here a group of the town's leaders is passing the Snigs Foot on their way to the parish church. Nearby is a bus stop — a reminder that Church Street was not pedestrianised at the time. Renfrey's the jeweller's shop and also the White Lion further down the road will be remembered by many. Now charity shops dominate the area.

The Regal Became Tesco's

What a pity that the town lost this cinema in 1963! Many townsfolk queued along the pavement to see such films as *The Doctor in Distress,* which was the last film to be shown there. The cinema had connections with royalty for it was where the Princess Royal received purses on behalf of the YMCA in 1949. Now, of course, Tesco's attracts the townsfolk to the same building.

Church House and the Charity School

There are very few views of the old charity school that was built in 1724 after Lord Derby and several local people subscribed to a fund to build the school in order to give children a means of avoiding poverty. There was opposition to the plan because it was feared that the poor would expect higher wages and become dissatisfied with servile work, while those in favour claimed that 'from such timely discipline the public may expect honest and industrious servants'. When the grammar school's building in the churchyard was condemned, the grammar school shared these premises until the school on Ruff Lane was built. Later the town library moved into the building. Now an alley between Tesco's and the old Church House marks its site.

The Church and Vicarage

The old vicarage stood on the site of New Church House. The building was very old; in fact when it was demolished the inner walls were found to be of lath and plaster. Since that time the church clock has been moved to a different position.

The Lane that Disappeared

A lane in front of the church used to lead down to some cottages where townsfolk used to gather to watch wedding parties as they approached the church. Now the remains of the lane skirt the new Church House and end in the garden, but a similar view of the church can be seen through the trees from the churchyard.

Coronation Park

Although this park is not on Church Street, it adjoins the churchyard and so is included here. Recently it has undergone an excellent modernisation programme. A play area with up-to-date equipment has been set up, bands play in the bandstand, teenagers skateboard on the play area and many festivals and other activities are staged here. It is a very attractive part of Ormskirk.

Burscough Street

The Opposite Side of the Street

Priory Carpets — once Woolworth's — and the Paper Box can be remembered by many in this view taken up the newly pedestrianised Burscough Street. Now it is dominated by the bright red façade of Pluck's, the bookmakers premises.

Coming and Going

Arthur's and Draper's were long-established businesses, but now Draper's has gone. Nevertheless the old building that at one time was Evans and Ball's, the provender merchants, remains the same and Arthur's continues to meet all the challenges from the market stalls and supermarkets.

The Jeweller's

Wainwright's too was an old established business that belonged to an Ormskirk family. The people who worked in these shops for many years became close friends of their customers, for instance townsfolk will long remember Phil Bottomley, the previous owner and Jack Bibby, the watchmaker in Wainwright's shop. Now the shop belongs to Joseph's, another jewellers, who carries on the same tradition.

The China Tea Establishment

No one will remember this shopkeeper or his shop, but nevertheless connections with his family continue in the Ormskirk area. This was the Evans family, who lived on St Helens Road and who had connections with the Emmanuel Methodist church. Later Mr Evans joined Mr Ball and became a partner in Evans and Ball's provender merchants. Now his former premises are among the most colourful in Ormskirk.

The Wheatsheaf

This was another of Ormskirk's prestigious inns, where the court leet, the local authority, often used to meet. Until the court was disbanded in 1875, it used to adjourn at the end of one session and plan a second session later in the year at the Wheatsheaf. It is tempting to wonder whether the reason was purely for the business of the court. When the inn was demolished, the new shopping development was called the Wheatsheaf Walk. *Inset:* the building of the Wheatsheaf Walk.

Swarbricks

This family had long connections with Ormskirk and particularly with the Mawdesley family, who had the grocer's shop near the clock in the early twentieth century. Gerard Swarbrick, who worked in the shop for forty-four years, tells that when the shop was opened, Mrs Connor was the first person to come through the doors to buy a pie. When the shop finally closed she was invited back to be the last person to make a purchase.

Up the Alleyway

Beside Swarbrick's shop was an alleyway leading to a cluster of old cottages and Mrs Connor lived in one of these. When the shop was redeveloped, the alleyway was enlarged and Swarbrick's opened a cheese shop in the newly-named Swan Alley. Now Swarbrick's two shops have gone and Church Walks leads to an attractive cluster of shops and cafés.

Mr Thomas' Shops

If Miss Mansergh's of Church Street could supply anything in the hardware line, Mr Thomas must have rivalled her. Seemingly while Mrs Thomas sold drapery in the left-hand side of the shop, her husband sold the hardware, brooms and brushes. It must have been difficult to get into the shop with all those products displayed on the pavement. Nowadays the flower shop also spills on to the pavement, but the railings have disappeared long ago.

The Sewing Machine Shop

What a different world — a shop devoted to selling one article and its accessories! All these shops could specialise in one aspect of trade and customers were happy to walk from one to another to find what they wanted. Within living memory the shop was divided into two premises, and the antique finishes were added to the façade.

The Tobacconist's Shop

Here is a business that has disappeared. Edie Culshaw, as she was affectionately known, was the last member of the Culshaw family to keep this shop that had been in the family for over a hundred years when she retired in 1976. All the trappings of a smoker's world were for sale — spills, pipes, tobacco and, of course, cigarettes. It seems ironic that a pharmacy, with its cures for tobacco-related illnesses, should occupy the premises now.

An Early Photographer

On the left is the shop of Wragg, the photographer, where part of the roof of the building was of glass to light the studio. Many old family photographs and *cartes de visites* of Ormskirk families were taken by Wragg. He must have been a rival of Mr Hardman, the Liverpool photographer whose studio now belongs to the National Trust. During the Second World War Bibby's the grocers had to paint the glass roof to comply with black-out regulations.

The Styles

Behind Burscough Street is the old stone house which appeared on the 1609 map. When it was renovated a piscina for holy water was found in one of the walls, suggesting that at one time the building may have been used as a chapel, possibly by the Catholics when they had to worship in secret. In recent times it was the workshop of Cobhams the basket makers. Now it has been converted into licensed premises.

The Corner of Burscough Street and Derby Street

The large house formerly belonged to the Heaton family and later became the surgery of first Dr Suffern and then Dr Temple. After the building was demolished, the site was used for the social services' offices and a car park before the construction of Ormskirk's police station transformed the site. The planners envisaged an open space in front of the building and certainly it enhances the appearance of the station.

The Library

Knowles House was opposite to the doctors' house. It was built by the Reverend Knowles for his wife in case she had to leave the vicarage after his death. However, she died first and it was not needed. Originally his garden stretched across what has become Derby Street. Later the house became the surgery of Dr Craig and Dr Pendlebury. It was an architectural gem, but was replaced by the library, that is not.

The Advertiser's Offices

A row of houses was demolished and this impressive office block was built for the local newspaper. It complements the architecture of the Farmers' Club, a building that was built to serve as the town's dispensary in 1832.

Aughton Street and Town End

Late Nineteenth Century Aughton Street

The upper photo was taken shortly after the clock tower was built in 1876 and before the Kings Arms was given its impressive frontage. Although the street is virtually empty, one lady is selling fish at the fish stones. The solitary gas lamp — supplied by the local gas works established in 1833 — increases the sense of desolation. By contrast today's Aughton Street is full of people enjoying the sunshine.

The Kings Arms and the Market

Now we can see two gas lamps, which would be lit to enable the market stallholders to continue in business long after dark. Some people can remember the stalls being lit by paraffin lamps and trading continuing into the night-time. When the second photo was taken, the grand Kings Arms had been replaced by flat-roofed shops that added nothing to the townscape and buses still wended their way around the market stalls.

Another View of the Market in the Early Twentieth Century

Mawdesley's, the original gingerbread shop, can be seen to the right of the clock tower and then comes the Fleece inn, which was demolished to make way for, what became, Barclays Bank. Although the next view was taken more recently, times have changed since then, for now cars and vans would not be allowed to pass down that part of Aughton Street.

Another Very Old Photograph of the Market Place

This old photo is fascinating. The inn on the corner of Aughton Street and Church Street, with shutters on the lower windows, was the George and Dragon, the next shop was W. Brown's drapery store, then the gable-ended shop was Lamberts the ironmonger's. According to the 1861 Census the very old property that came next was the home of a master cooper, James Arrowsmith, while between the last two houses — probably up the alleyway — lived Richard Winrow, a roper who employed twelve men and twenty boys. The last building in the photo was Garside's shop, which continued in the same place for many years. What a difference today!

Looking Towards the Talbot Hotel

Further down the street was the grand Talbot Hotel that had a stable yard where travellers could stable their horses. In 1790 a visitor wrote 'scarcely had we alighted at the Talbot Inn when we were offered by half a dozen fair hands together, little packets of gingerbread'. Evidently Ormskirk's gingerbreads — and young ladies — were famous as early as the 1700s. Now the Talbot has been demolished to make way for more shops but gingerbreads are still sold in the town.

OMK 110 Market and Clock Tower, Ormskirk

More Demolition

Although the building that is the coffee house between Barclays and the Abbey National looks old, this postcard shows that the original building — once Mawdesley's grocers — was demolished completely. The developer of that site was sympathetic to the old townscape and put up a new building that looks very similar to its predecessor.

Behind Aughton Street

In the 1920s these cottages stood behind a large building known as Troqueer Building, which was opposite the site of Morrison's supermarket. The houses probably date from the time when farmland stretched up the hill behind the houses. They certainly look like farm cottages, probably both built of local stone. When they were demolished other residential properties, such as the houses on the road at the side of Hesford's store, were built on the site.

More Cottages

According to the 1881 Census, there were over twenty of these courts off Aughton Street and some had as many as twenty-one separate dwellings around them. No wonder there were epidemics when people lived in such crowded conditions! Again the sites are being used as car parks.

On the Site of Morrison's

These large houses were lodging houses where many Irish immigrants lived after they left their homeland to escape from the famine. The gateposts marked the entrance to 'Fogg's' chapel, so-called because the Reverend Fogg was minister there for many years. He followed the tradition of Nathaniel Heywood, the Puritan, who was ejected from the parish church in 1662. The Fogg family's gravestone is in the pavement alongside Morrison's side entrance.

Outside the Old Sweet Shop
Here we are looking back at the Greyhound pub and those same lodging houses. Now the site of the whole row is part of Morrison's supermarket.

EDWARD SUDBURY,
ALE AND PORTER BREWER,
AUGHTON BREWERY, **ORMSKIRK.**

An Amazing Advertisement

The family, who once lived at Town End Cottage at the corner of Aughton Street and Prescot Road, have this advertisement for Forshaw's brewery at Town End. It dates from the nineteenth century and the drawing of the brewery chimney belching smoke, the carriages and carts give a glimpse of that period. There was no County Road and there were no houses on Holborn Hill; now that triangle of land is covered with residential property. *Inset:* Town End Cottage.

Cows on Aughton Street

Another drawing dated 1877 shows Town End from Dyer's Lane. The tower of St Anne's church and the windmill on the top of Holborn Hill can be seen. Cows are grazing in the fields where the houses on Prescot Road stand today.

St Anne's Church

This postcard confirms that cattle grazed in the fields near St Anne's church. St Bede's Catholic School was built on that grassland at the corner of Prescot Road and St Anne's Road.

Another View of Town End

The row of cottages in this photo was demolished to make way for St Anne's social centre, a very popular venue for all kinds of social activities. Many years ago Father Bulmer's presbytery and later St Oswald's Catholic church stood on this plot of land, and the Catholic school was on the same site before it moved to Hants Lane.

The Clock Tower

During the war the clock tower was used to publicise the National Savings campaign. It is not surprising that at that time, when things were in short supply, the market had reduced in size. Since then the number of stalls grouped around the clock tower has doubled or even trebled as the stalls became more attractive and visits to the market became more popular.

Other Streets in the Town

The Church from Derby Street West

The church broods over an ever-increasing traffic problem. The vibrations caused by the lorries that trundle past so close to the walls of the old church, cause plaster to fall from the walls, and it is possible that one day the church will collapse and the town will lose a unique part of its heritage. The narrow road also causes endless traffic jams, but the bypass is still deferred year after year.

The Old Fire Station

This faint view of the old fire station seems to be all that is available. The station was built when the fire engine was pulled by horses, which were stabled further down the road behind what was then the Commercial Hotel. When the fire bell rang, volunteers ran to fetch the horses and bring them to the station. Now the site is yet another car park and the engines are housed at Town End.

Ormskirk Firemen Through the Years

The fire brigade, photographed in 1934. It must have taken them a long time to don their helmets, boots and buttoned uniforms. Today's uniform is certainly 'quick fit for purpose'. The chairman of the council, William Burrows, is in a bowler hat while his chauffeur is holding the bell. The engine was a Daimler Benze and was the first motorised fire engine used in Ormskirk. How different from today's monsters!

More Firemen

This fire crew are grouped in front of the old Mary Rose restaurant that became the fire station in 1956 when it was taken over from the military authorities. They are, at the back: Jim Cave, Jack Cheetham, Frank Duckett, Jack Sadgrove, Dick Wright, Pater Judd, Alf Ball. In front are Norman Sheen, Dick Ashcroft, Jack Stevenon, John Morris, Jack Rawsthorne, Sid Wareing, Arthur Raynor. Below is today's station.

The Elms

This building has changed very little in appearance over the years. It was the home of Mr Marples, J.P., and the lady in front of the old photograph was named as Miss Wiseman. Later the house became Dr Craig's surgery and now a dentist uses the premises.

Unchanged Derby Street

Very little has altered in the appearance of Derby Street. The only noticeable thing is the method of transport and the loss of the iron railings that were collected for the war effort during the Second World War. Nevertheless, if the appearance of the buildings has not changed, their owners and uses have. A major change came when the school closed and the building was sold to Stokers to be a furniture store.

Waterworks

In the 1850s Ormskirk had a severe health crisis, mainly the result of drinking polluted water from wells that either had not been sunk to a sufficient depth or were too close to pigsties, privies or refuse dumps. A board of health was formed, wells were dug and pumping stations built to supply the town. The Greetby Hill water tower was an early one and was followed by the one on Tower Hill, which is now awaiting redevelopment.

The Mushroom
The waterworks that now supply water to the locality has a tower shaped like a mushroom that can be seen for miles around. The previous one on the site was less obtrusive.

The Scouts

This year (2009) the 1st Ormskirk Scouts were proud to celebrate their centenary, and their banner was restored as part of the celebrations. The old photograph was taken shortly after their formation and it is thought that the group included Baden-Powell, while the man not in uniform was Lord Derby. Now girls are included in the troop and they feature in the lower photograph.

The Workhouse

The Victorian workhouse was built in 1853 to replace the one housed in three cottages in Moor Street End. The first workhouse was in Aughton Street, where it was founded in 1732. Although the workhouse became Ormskirk County Hospital, it was not until 1960 that the last of the people who had lived in the old workhouse were finally housed elsewhere. Now Ormskirk has a wonderful new hospital, and one wing of the old structure waits to be demolished.

The Grammar School

Here the grammar school is being demolished to make way for a housing development. The grammar school was founded in a small building in the parish churchyard in 1612 and moved to this site in 1850. Over the years extensions, such as these buildings, were added as the grammar school's reputation grew. Later it became a comprehensive school and recently was amalgamated with Cross Hall High School in a state-of-the-art building. It is now called Ormskirk School.

Edge Hill University

Edge Hill training college was founded in Liverpool and moved to Ormskirk in 1933. It was evacuated to Bingley during the war when the building was requisitioned for use as a hospital for the forces. Now as one of the new universities it is expanding rapidly. Each year more residential accommodation is built and new laboratories and lecture theatres — and car parks — are added to the site. Now a special bus serves the university.

Chapel Street

Most of the courts off Chapel Street have been demolished. However, one side of court number seven has been upgraded and provides a secluded site for several small homes.

Elm Place

This is another of the photographs taken when the council was examining property that they thought was below standard in the town. The old washtub, the mangle, the hen scratching in the yard, the old pram and the outside privy paint a picture of what life was like in those cottages in the 1920s. Again, they have been upgraded and are now an attractive terrace of small houses.

The Clinic

The clinic was built in 1958 on part of 'The Peace', a field that was left by Mr Marple, J.P., in 1935 for the children of Ormskirk. The council exchanged the land for a playing field in Green Lane, but at the time the townsfolk were disappointed to lose such an amenity so close to the town centre. Evidently the authorities decided that a clinic would serve the children better than a playing field.

Hants Lane

This row of cottages led off Hants Lane near Martin Square between Green Lane and the children's field. During the late nineteenth and early twentieth centuries most of the people who lived there were Irish and had immigrated to England during the aftermath of the famine. The whole area was redeveloped, and pensioners' bungalows now occupy the same site.

Pennington Avenue

Another row of old cottages that have been replaced by Pennington Avenue. Some of the old walling still exists at the side of the road.

Green Lane

These cottages have also gone and have been replaced by modern housing. They were the homes of large families, but the only one that I can name is the Shorlicar family who lived in the last house. Perhaps someone will be able to name them all and complete the record. The strange chimneys showing behind the houses were on the malt house that was at the rear of Southport Road.

More Green Lane
These back yards were also on Green Lane, possibly belonging to the same cottages. Again they give us a glimpse of life in the town in the 1920s, when many people still lived in those conditions. The privies against the wall suggest that they were not water closets but dry ones that were emptied by the cart that cleared all the middens at certain intervals.

Cottage Lane Mission

The old mission, built in the style of so many churches, brings back memories, but nevertheless there are many churchgoers who wish that they had a modern building like this one with up-to-date facilities and an attractive appearance.

Goodbye to Ormskirk
A glimpse of its unique church, with both a tower and steeple at
the western end of the building.

Acknowledgements

I want to acknowledge the debt I owe to Dennis Walton, the
talented photographer who has taken most of the colour
photographs in this book. It has been a pleasure to work
with him. I want to thank my friend June Bibby for the
help she has given me in researching the past in Ormskirk,
and also West Lancashire Borough Council and the many
friends who have contributed their precious photographs
to my collection. Thank you all for helping to produce this
fascinating review of Ormskirk through time.